Zermatt travel Guide 2024/2025

Insider Tips and Must – see Attractions

Ruby P. Philip

Copyright © 2024 by Ruby P. Philip

All rights reserved. No part of this publication may be reproduced, distributed, or transmitted in any form or by any means, including photocopying, recording, or other electronic or mechanical methods, without the prior written permission of the publisher, except in the case of brief quotations embodied in critical reviews and certain other noncommercial uses permitted by copyright law.

Disclaimer

The information in this book is provided as a guide to assist travelers in planning their trips to Zermatt. While every effort has been made to ensure the accuracy and completeness of the information contained within, the author and publisher make no representations or warranties of any kind, express or implied, about the completeness, accuracy, reliability, suitability, or availability with respect to the book or the information, products, services, or related graphics contained in the book for any purpose. Any reliance you place on such information is therefore strictly at your own risk.

Through this book, you are able to link to other websites which are not under the control of the author or publisher. We have no control over the nature, content, and availability of those sites. The inclusion of any links does not necessarily imply a recommendation or endorse the views expressed within them.

Every effort is made to keep the book up and running smoothly. However, the author and publisher take no responsibility for, and will not be liable for, the book being temporarily unavailable due to technical issues beyond our control.

Contents

Chapter 1: Introduction to Zermatt 7
Overview of Zermatt 7
History and Background 9
Unique Features of Zermatt 12

Chapter 2: Planning Your Trip 17
Researching Your Destination 17
Setting Your Travel Goals 20
Creating an Itinerary 24

Chapter 3: When to Visit 31
Seasonal Highlights 31
Best Time for Outdoor Activities 34
Weather Considerations 38

Chapter 4: Budgeting for Your Trip 41
Estimating Costs 41
Saving Tips 45
Affordable Accommodation and Dining Options 48

Chapter 5: Essentials for Traveling 52
Packing List 52
Health and Safety Tips 56
Travel Insurance 58

Chapter 6: Entry and Visa Requirements 63
Visa Information for Different Nationalities 63
Customs Regulations 66

Important Travel Documents 69

Chapter 7: Getting to Zermatt **73**

Transportation Options 73

Navigating Airports and Train Stations 77

Local Transportation in Zermatt 80

Chapter 8: Accommodation in Zermatt **85**

Types of Accommodation 85

Choosing the Right Area 89

Booking Tips 92

Chapter 9: Cultural Experiences **97**

Local Traditions and Festivals 97

Cuisine and Dining Experiences 100

Museums and Historical Sites 104

Chapter 10: Accommodation in Zermatt **110**

Luxury Hotels 110

Budget-Friendly Hotels 112

Restaurants in Zermatt 114

Chapter 11: Five-Day Itinerary for Zermatt **117**

Day 1: Arrival and Exploration 117

Day 2: Skiing and Adventure 118

Day 3: Glacier Paradise and Hiking 119

Day 4: Relaxation and Sightseeing 120

Day 5: Departure and Last-minute Exploration 121

Chapter 12: Outdoor Activities & Attractions **123**

Skiing and Snowboarding 123

Hiking and Mountain Climbing 125

Exploring the Matterhorn and Other Natural Wonders...... 128

Chapter 1: Introduction to Zermatt

Overview of Zermatt

Nestled in the heart of the Swiss Alps, Zermatt is a charming mountain village renowned for its breathtaking landscapes, world-class skiing, and iconic views of the Matterhorn. This car-free resort town, situated in the German-speaking region of the canton of Valais, offers a perfect blend of natural beauty, outdoor adventure, and Swiss hospitality.

Zermatt's elevation at 1,620 meters (5,315 feet) above sea level ensures a picturesque alpine setting, characterized by pristine snow-covered peaks in winter and lush green valleys in summer. The town itself is a delightful mix of traditional Swiss chalets and modern amenities, making it a popular destination for tourists seeking both adventure and relaxation.

The town is easily accessible by train, with the Matterhorn Gotthard Bahn providing scenic journeys through the mountains. For those arriving by car, parking is available in the nearby village of Täsch, with shuttle services to Zermatt. This unique aspect of Zermatt—its commitment to being car-free—contributes to its tranquil atmosphere and unspoiled environment.

Zermatt is not just about its stunning surroundings; it is also a hub for winter sports enthusiasts. The area boasts some of the best skiing and snowboarding slopes in the world, attracting professionals and amateurs alike. With over 360 kilometers (224 miles) of ski runs, the resort offers a variety of terrains suitable for all skill levels. During the summer months, the town transforms into a hiker's paradise, with numerous trails leading to breathtaking viewpoints and alpine lakes.

The vibrant town center is filled with shops, restaurants, and bars, offering everything from traditional Swiss cuisine to international delicacies. The local culture is deeply rooted in alpine traditions, which are celebrated through various festivals and events throughout the year. Visitors can explore the rich history of the region by visiting the Matterhorn Museum, which provides insights into the development of alpinism and the local way of life.

History and Background

The history of Zermatt is closely linked to the development of mountaineering and tourism in the Swiss Alps. Originally a modest farming village, Zermatt began to gain prominence in the mid-19th century when adventurers and explorers from around the world started to flock to the region to conquer the Matterhorn.

The Matterhorn, standing at 4,478 meters (14,692 feet), is one of the most famous mountains in the world. Its distinctive pyramid shape and challenging climbing routes have made it a symbol of the Swiss Alps. The first successful ascent of the Matterhorn in 1865 by a team led by Edward Whymper marked a significant milestone in the history of alpinism and put Zermatt on the map as a key destination for climbers.

The village's transformation into a tourist hub accelerated with the arrival of the railway in 1891, making Zermatt more accessible to visitors. The construction of luxurious hotels and the development of ski lifts and other infrastructure further boosted its popularity. The town's commitment to preserving its natural beauty and traditional charm, while embracing modern amenities, has made it a unique destination that attracts millions of visitors each year.

Zermatt has also been at the forefront of environmental conservation efforts. The decision to ban cars from the town center was made in the 1960s to combat pollution and preserve the pristine alpine environment. This move has been highly successful, contributing to Zermatt's reputation as a clean and sustainable destination.

Over the years, Zermatt has continued to evolve, blending its rich historical heritage with contemporary tourism trends. The town has hosted numerous international events, including the prestigious Zermatt Unplugged music festival and the Patrouille des Glaciers, one of the world's most challenging ski mountaineering races. These events, along with its natural attractions, ensure that Zermatt remains a vibrant and dynamic destination.

Unique Features of Zermatt

Zermatt's allure lies in its unique combination of natural beauty, outdoor adventure, and cultural richness. One of the most distinctive features of Zermatt is its car-free policy. By prohibiting motor vehicles, the town has maintained a peaceful and unpolluted environment, allowing visitors to enjoy the pristine alpine air and stunning vistas without the noise and fumes of traffic. Electric taxis and horse-drawn carriages provide charming and eco-friendly transportation within the town.

The Matterhorn, often referred to as the "Mountain of Mountains," is undoubtedly Zermatt's most iconic feature. Its majestic presence dominates the landscape, offering unparalleled opportunities for photography, climbing, and exploration. The Gornergrat Railway, one of the highest cogwheel railways in Europe, provides easy access to breathtaking views of the Matterhorn and the surrounding peaks. This scenic train journey is a must-do for visitors, offering a unique perspective of the alpine environment.

Zermatt is also home to the Matterhorn Glacier Paradise, the highest cable car station in Europe at 3,883 meters (12,739 feet). This remarkable attraction allows visitors to experience the wonders of the glacier, including an ice palace and panoramic views of the Swiss, Italian, and French Alps. The year-round snow conditions make it possible to ski and snowboard even in summer, attracting winter sports enthusiasts from around the globe.

The town's dedication to sustainability and conservation is another standout feature. Zermatt's commitment to renewable energy, waste reduction, and preservation of natural resources has earned it recognition as a model of sustainable tourism. The local government and businesses actively promote eco-friendly practices, ensuring that the region's natural beauty is protected for future generations.

Zermatt's culinary scene is a delightful fusion of traditional Swiss cuisine and international flavors. From cozy mountain huts serving hearty alpine dishes to Michelin-starred restaurants offering gourmet experiences, there is something to satisfy every palate. Local specialties such as raclette, fondue, and dried meats are a must-try for food enthusiasts.

The town's rich cultural heritage is celebrated through various events and festivals. The Zermatt Unplugged music festival, held annually in April, features acoustic performances by renowned artists in intimate settings, creating a unique and memorable experience. The Folklore Festival, held in August, showcases traditional Swiss music, dance, and crafts, providing a glimpse into the region's vibrant culture.

Zermatt's commitment to offering a diverse range of activities ensures that there is something for everyone. In addition to skiing and hiking, visitors can enjoy mountain biking, paragliding, and climbing. The town also offers wellness and spa facilities, providing relaxation and rejuvenation after a day of adventure.

In conclusion, Zermatt is a destination that captivates the senses and offers a unique blend of natural wonders, cultural experiences, and sustainable tourism practices. Its iconic

Matterhorn, commitment to environmental preservation, and rich history make it a must-visit location for travelers seeking both adventure and tranquility in the heart of the Swiss Alps.

Chapter 2: Planning Your Trip

Researching Your Destination

Researching your destination is the first crucial step in planning a successful trip to Zermatt. Thorough research can enhance your experience, ensuring that you are well-prepared and able to make the most of your visit to this stunning alpine village.

Understanding Zermatt's Geography and Climate

Zermatt is located in the German-speaking part of the canton of Valais in Switzerland, at an elevation of 1,620 meters (5,315 feet) above sea level. The town is nestled at the foot of the Matterhorn, one of the most iconic and photographed mountains in the world. Understanding the geography of Zermatt will help you plan your activities and prepare for the weather conditions you might encounter.

The climate in Zermatt varies significantly with the seasons. Winter, from December to March, is characterized by heavy snowfall and cold temperatures, making it a paradise for skiers and snowboarders. Summer, from June to September, offers mild temperatures and clear skies, ideal for hiking and outdoor activities. Spring and autumn are transitional seasons with fewer tourists, offering a more serene experience.

Accommodation Options

Researching accommodation options in Zermatt is essential as the town offers a wide range of lodging choices, from luxurious hotels to budget-friendly hostels. Consider factors such as location, amenities, and price when choosing your accommodation. Staying close to the town center will provide easy access to shops, restaurants, and transportation, while accommodations further out may offer more tranquility and stunning views of the Matterhorn.

Activities and Attractions

Zermatt is renowned for its outdoor activities, particularly skiing and hiking. Research the various ski resorts, hiking trails, and other attractions to determine which ones best suit your interests and skill levels. Popular attractions include the Gornergrat Railway, the Matterhorn Glacier Paradise, and the Matterhorn Museum. Familiarize yourself with the opening hours, ticket prices, and any seasonal restrictions for these attractions.

Understanding local customs and etiquette can enhance your experience and help you interact more comfortably with the residents. Swiss culture is known for its punctuality, cleanliness, and respect for privacy. Learning a few basic German phrases, as it is the predominant language in

Zermatt, can also be beneficial and appreciated by the locals.

Researching safety and health considerations is crucial, especially when traveling to high-altitude destinations like Zermatt. Be aware of the symptoms of altitude sickness and take necessary precautions. Additionally, ensure you have adequate travel insurance that covers medical emergencies and outdoor activities. Familiarize yourself with the location of medical facilities in Zermatt and any health advisories or vaccination requirements.

Zermatt is a car-free town, so understanding the transportation options is essential. The primary mode of transportation to Zermatt is by train, with the Matterhorn Gotthard Bahn providing scenic routes. If you are driving, you will need to park your car in Täsch and take a shuttle train or taxi to Zermatt. Within the town, electric taxis, buses, and horse-drawn carriages are available for getting around.

Setting clear travel goals will help you focus your trip planning efforts and ensure that your visit to Zermatt aligns with your interests and expectations. Here are some steps to help you define and achieve your travel goals:

Start by identifying your interests and priorities. Are you an adventure seeker looking to conquer the slopes and trails, or are you seeking relaxation and cultural experiences? Zermatt offers a diverse range of activities, so knowing what excites you will help you plan accordingly. List your top interests, such as skiing, hiking, exploring local cuisine, or immersing yourself in Swiss culture.

Determine the Purpose of Your Trip

Understanding the purpose of your trip can further refine your travel goals. Are you traveling for a romantic getaway, a family vacation, or a solo adventure? Each type of trip may have different priorities and requirements. For instance, a family vacation may focus on kid-friendly activities and accommodations, while a solo adventure might prioritize challenging hiking trails and personal growth experiences.

Setting realistic and specific goals will help you make the most of your time in Zermatt. Instead of vague goals like "have fun" or "explore," try to be more specific. For example, you might set a goal to "ski the Sunnegga Paradise slopes," "hike to the Hörnlihütte for a close-up view of the Matterhorn," or "attend the Zermatt Unplugged music festival." Specific goals provide clear direction and make it easier to plan your activities.

While it's tempting to fill your itinerary with back-to-back activities, it's important to balance your schedule with downtime. Overpacking your itinerary can lead to exhaustion and prevent you from fully enjoying your experiences. Set goals that include time for relaxation, such as enjoying a leisurely meal at a mountain hut, exploring the town at your own pace, or simply soaking in the breathtaking views.

Your travel goals may vary depending on the season you visit Zermatt. In winter, your goals might focus on skiing, snowboarding, and winter sports, while in summer, you might aim to explore hiking trails, mountain biking, and outdoor festivals. Understanding the seasonal offerings of Zermatt will help you set goals that align with the best activities available during your visit.

Traveling is an opportunity for learning and personal growth. Consider setting goals that allow you to expand your horizons and learn new skills. For example, you might set a goal to take a mountaineering course, learn about Swiss cheese-making, or practice speaking German with locals. These experiences can enrich your trip and provide lasting memories.

If you're traveling with others, involve them in the goal-setting process. Discuss each person's interests and preferences to ensure that everyone's expectations are considered. Collaborative goal-setting can lead to a more harmonious trip and ensure that everyone has a fulfilling experience. Create a list of shared goals as well as individual ones to accommodate different interests.

While setting goals is important, it's equally important to stay flexible and open-minded. Unexpected opportunities and spontaneous experiences often make the best travel memories. Be prepared to adapt your plans if necessary and embrace the unexpected moments that come your way. Flexibility allows you to make the most of your trip, even if things don't go exactly as planned.

Creating an Itinerary

Creating a well-structured itinerary is key to making the most of your trip to Zermatt. An effective itinerary helps you organize your time, ensures you don't miss out on key experiences, and allows for a smooth and enjoyable travel experience. Here are some steps to guide you in creating an itinerary for your Zermatt adventure:

Start with a Rough Outline

Begin by creating a rough outline of your trip, including your arrival and departure dates. Note down the main activities or attractions you want to visit on each day. This initial outline will give you a framework to build upon and help you visualize your overall schedule.

Allocate Time for Travel and Logistics

Factor in time for travel and logistics, including your journey to Zermatt, checking in and out of accommodations, and transportation within the town. Consider the time it takes to get from one activity or attraction to another. For instance, if you're taking the Gornergrat Railway to the summit, account for travel time, waiting periods, and the duration of your visit.

Prioritize Key Activities

Identify the key activities or attractions that are must-dos for your trip and prioritize them in your itinerary. These might include skiing at specific resorts, hiking certain trails, visiting the Matterhorn Museum, or taking a scenic train ride. Schedule these activities first to ensure they fit into your plan.

Plan for Peak Times and Reservations

Some activities and attractions in Zermatt may require advance reservations, especially during peak tourist seasons. For example, dining at popular restaurants, booking ski lessons, or securing spots on guided tours may need to be arranged in advance. Research and make necessary reservations early to avoid disappointment.

Balance Activities with Rest

A well-balanced itinerary includes both activities and rest periods. Plan for downtime between activities to relax, enjoy meals, and explore the town at a leisurely pace. Overloading your schedule can lead to fatigue and diminish the enjoyment of your trip. Ensure you have time to rest and recharge.

Consider Weather and Seasonal Factors

Weather can significantly impact your plans, especially in a mountainous region like Zermatt. Check the weather forecast regularly and have a contingency plan for indoor activities in case of bad weather. Seasonal factors, such as snowfall in winter or trail conditions in summer, should also be considered when planning your activities.

Incorporate Local Events and Festivals

Zermatt hosts various events and festivals throughout the year, such as the Zermatt

Unplugged music festival and the Folklore Festival. Check the local event calendar and incorporate these into your itinerary if they align with your travel dates. Attending local events can provide unique cultural experiences and enrich your trip.

Leave Room for Spontaneity

While having a structured itinerary is helpful, leaving some room for spontaneity is equally important. Allow for flexible time slots where you can explore unexpected opportunities, discover hidden gems, or simply relax and soak in the atmosphere. Spontaneous moments often create the most memorable experiences.

Review and Adjust Your Itinerary

Before finalizing your itinerary, review it to ensure it is realistic and achievable. Consider factors such as travel time, opening hours of attractions, and your own energy levels. Make adjustments as needed to avoid overloading any single day. A

well-paced itinerary enhances the overall
enjoyment of your trip.

Share Your Itinerary

If you're traveling with others, share your itinerary
with them and gather feedback. Ensure that
everyone is aware of the plan and agrees with the
schedule. Sharing your itinerary with a trusted
friend or family member who is not traveling with
you can also be a good safety precaution.

Pack Accordingly

Finally, use your itinerary to guide your packing.
Ensure you have appropriate clothing and gear for
each activity, such as ski equipment, hiking boots,
and weather-appropriate clothing. Having the right
gear will ensure you are prepared for all planned
activities and can fully enjoy your experiences.

Planning your trip to Zermatt involves thorough
research, setting clear travel goals, and creating a
well-structured itinerary. By understanding your

destination, defining your interests and priorities, and organizing your time effectively, you can ensure a memorable and fulfilling visit to this breathtaking alpine village. Whether you're seeking adventure, relaxation, or cultural enrichment, a well-planned trip to Zermatt promises an unforgettable experience in the heart of the Swiss Alps.

Chapter 3: When to Visit

Seasonal Highlights

Zermatt is a year-round destination, with each season offering its own unique highlights and attractions. Understanding the seasonal changes and the best activities during each period can help you decide when to visit this enchanting alpine village.

Winter (December to February)

Winter in Zermatt is a magical time, transforming the town into a winter wonderland. This season is characterized by heavy snowfall, making it a paradise for winter sports enthusiasts. The snow-covered landscape provides the perfect backdrop for skiing, snowboarding, and other winter activities. Zermatt boasts one of the largest and highest ski areas in Europe, with over 360 kilometers (224 miles) of pistes, ensuring plenty of options for skiers of all levels.

One of the major highlights of winter is the Zermatt Unplugged music festival, which takes place in April but often begins preparations during the winter months. This acoustic music festival attracts international artists and offers intimate performances in various venues around the town, creating a unique and festive atmosphere.

Spring (March to May)
Spring in Zermatt is a transitional season, with the landscape gradually transforming from snowy white to lush green. This period is less crowded, providing a more serene and peaceful experience. As the snow begins to melt, lower-altitude hiking trails open up, allowing visitors to explore the picturesque surroundings.

Spring is also a great time for skiing, especially in the early months. The higher-altitude slopes still have excellent snow conditions, and the warmer temperatures make for more comfortable skiing.

Additionally, this is the season when you can enjoy both winter and early summer activities, offering a unique combination for outdoor enthusiasts.

Summer (June to August)

Summer in Zermatt is characterized by warm temperatures, clear skies, and lush green landscapes. This season is ideal for outdoor activities such as hiking, mountain biking, and climbing. Zermatt offers an extensive network of hiking trails, ranging from easy walks to challenging alpine routes. Popular trails include the Gornergrat, which provides stunning views of the Matterhorn, and the Five Lakes Walk, which takes you past five beautiful mountain lakes.

The summer months also bring a range of festivals and events, such as the Zermatt Folklore Festival in August. This festival celebrates Swiss traditions with music, dance, and local crafts, offering visitors a glimpse into the region's rich cultural heritage.

Autumn (September to November)

Autumn in Zermatt is another transitional period, with the landscape showcasing a stunning array of fall colors. The weather is generally mild, making it an excellent time for hiking and outdoor exploration. The trails are less crowded, allowing for a more tranquil experience.

This season is also perfect for photography, as the changing leaves and clear skies provide beautiful backdrops for capturing the alpine scenery. Additionally, autumn is the harvest season, and you can enjoy local food festivals and culinary events that highlight regional specialties.

Best Time for Outdoor Activities

Zermatt is renowned for its outdoor activities, which vary depending on the season. Here's a guide to the best time for various outdoor pursuits:

Skiing and Snowboarding

The best time for skiing and snowboarding in Zermatt is from December to April. The winter months offer the most reliable snow conditions, with January and February being the peak months for snowfall. The higher-altitude slopes of Zermatt, including the Matterhorn Glacier Paradise, allow for skiing even in the summer, although the winter season provides the most extensive options.

Hiking and Trekking

Summer (June to August) is the prime season for hiking and trekking in Zermatt. The trails are fully accessible, and the weather is warm and pleasant. Late spring and early autumn also offer excellent hiking conditions, with fewer crowds and stunning natural scenery. Popular hikes include the Gornergrat, the Höhbalmen trail, and the walk to the Hörnlihütte, the base camp for climbers attempting the Matterhorn ascent.

Mountain Biking

Mountain biking enthusiasts will find the best conditions from June to September. Zermatt offers a variety of trails catering to different skill levels, from gentle paths to challenging downhill routes. The Bike Park Zermatt, with its well-maintained trails and breathtaking views, is a must-visit for bikers. Additionally, the annual Zermatt Marathon in July draws athletes from around the world, providing both competitive and recreational mountain biking experiences.

Climbing and Mountaineering

The climbing and mountaineering season in Zermatt runs from late June to early September. The Matterhorn, one of the most iconic mountains in the world, attracts climbers eager to conquer its challenging routes. Summer provides the best conditions for climbing, with stable weather and less snow on the higher peaks. Guided climbs are recommended for those unfamiliar with the terrain, and there are several local companies offering professional mountaineering services.

Paragliding

Paragliding is a popular activity in Zermatt, offering a unique perspective of the alpine landscape. The best time for paragliding is from June to September, when the weather is most conducive to flying. Tandem flights are available for beginners, providing an exhilarating experience with stunning aerial views of the Matterhorn and surrounding mountains.

Trail Running

For those who enjoy running, Zermatt offers numerous trails suitable for trail running. The summer months (June to August) are ideal, with mild temperatures and clear paths. The annual Matterhorn Ultraks in August is a major event, attracting trail runners from around the globe to compete in various race categories amidst the spectacular alpine scenery.

Weather Considerations

Understanding the weather patterns in Zermatt is essential for planning your trip and ensuring a safe and enjoyable experience. Here's a detailed look at the weather considerations for each season:

Winter Weather (December to February)
Winter in Zermatt is characterized by cold temperatures and heavy snowfall. Average temperatures range from -10°C to 2°C (14°F to 36°F). The heavy snowfall creates excellent conditions for skiing and snowboarding but can also lead to occasional disruptions in transportation and accessibility. It's important to dress in layers, wear appropriate winter gear, and stay informed about weather forecasts and avalanche warnings.

Spring Weather (March to May)

Spring in Zermatt sees a gradual warming of temperatures, ranging from -5°C to 10°C (23°F to 50°F) in March and rising to 5°C to 15°C (41°F to 59°F) by May. The snow begins to melt, especially at lower altitudes, leading to mixed conditions on trails and slopes. Waterproof footwear and layered clothing are recommended, as weather can be unpredictable with occasional rain and snow showers.

Summer Weather (June to August)

Summer is the warmest season in Zermatt, with temperatures ranging from 10°C to 25°C (50°F to 77°F). Clear skies and long daylight hours make it perfect for outdoor activities. However, temperatures can drop significantly at higher altitudes, so it's advisable to carry warm clothing even in summer. Afternoon thunderstorms are not uncommon, so it's best to start activities early in the day and be prepared for sudden weather changes.

Autumn Weather (September to November)

Autumn sees a drop in temperatures, ranging from 5°C to 20°C (41°F to 68°F) in September and 0°C to 10°C (32°F to 50°F) by November. The weather is generally mild and stable, but temperatures can vary widely, especially in the mountains. Dressing in layers is essential, and be prepared for cooler temperatures and potential early snowfall in November.

General Weather Tips

- Altitude Effects: Zermatt is located at a high altitude, and weather conditions can change rapidly. Be prepared for sudden drops in temperature and strong winds, especially when venturing into higher elevations.
- UV Protection: Due to the high altitude, UV radiation is stronger. Wear sunscreen, sunglasses, and a hat to protect yourself from sunburn, even on cloudy days.
- Hydration: The dry alpine air can lead to dehydration. Drink plenty of water,

especially when engaging in physical activities.
- Weather Forecasts: Regularly check weather forecasts from reliable sources. Local tourist offices and accommodation providers can offer up-to-date weather information and advice.

Deciding when to visit Zermatt depends largely on your interests and preferred activities. Each season offers its own unique charm and opportunities, from the winter wonderland ideal for skiing to the lush summer landscapes perfect for hiking and mountain biking. Understanding the seasonal highlights, the best times for various outdoor activities, and weather considerations will help you plan a memorable trip to Zermatt. Whether you seek adventure, relaxation, or cultural experiences, Zermatt's breathtaking alpine scenery and diverse offerings ensure a fulfilling visit year-round.

Chapter 4: Budgeting for Your Trip

Estimating Costs

Planning a trip to Zermatt involves careful budgeting to ensure that you can enjoy all the experiences this beautiful alpine village has to offer without overspending. Here's a breakdown of the main costs to consider:

Accommodation

Accommodation in Zermatt can range from luxurious five-star hotels to budget-friendly hostels. On average, you can expect to spend around CHF 200-400 per night for a mid-range hotel. Luxury hotels can cost upwards of CHF 500 per night, while budget accommodations like hostels or guesthouses might be available for CHF 50-100 per night. Booking well in advance can help secure better rates.

Transportation

Zermatt is a car-free town, so you'll need to factor in the cost of transportation to and within the village. The most common way to reach Zermatt is by train. A round-trip ticket from Zurich to Zermatt costs approximately CHF 150-200 in second class. Once in Zermatt, local transportation options include electric taxis and buses, which are reasonably priced at around CHF 10-20 per trip. A Swiss Travel Pass might be a cost-effective option if you plan to explore other parts of Switzerland as well.

Food and Dining

Dining in Zermatt can be pricey, especially if you frequent upscale restaurants. A meal at a mid-range restaurant can cost around CHF 30-50 per person, while fine dining establishments might charge CHF 100 or more per meal. For budget-conscious travelers, cheaper options such as cafes, bakeries,

and fast food outlets are available, with meals
costing around CHF 10-20.

Activities and Attractions

Zermatt offers a wide range of activities, from
skiing and snowboarding to hiking and sightseeing.
A ski pass for the Zermatt ski area costs around
CHF 75-100 per day, depending on the season. The
Gornergrat Railway, a popular attraction, charges
around CHF 90 for a round trip. Entry fees for
museums and other attractions are generally more
affordable, ranging from CHF 10-20.

Miscellaneous Costs

Additional costs to consider include travel
insurance, souvenirs, and incidental expenses such
as tips and local taxes. Travel insurance is highly
recommended and typically costs around 4-8% of
your total trip cost. Budgeting an extra CHF 20-50
per day for miscellaneous expenses can help cover
unexpected costs.

Saving Tips

Traveling to Zermatt doesn't have to break the bank. Here are some tips to help you save money while still enjoying a memorable trip:

Travel During the Off-Season
Visiting Zermatt during the shoulder seasons (spring and autumn) can result in significant savings on accommodation and flights. These periods are less crowded, and many hotels offer discounted rates. Additionally, you can enjoy a more tranquil experience with fewer tourists.

Book in Advance
Booking your accommodation, transportation, and activities well in advance can secure lower rates and availability. Early bird discounts are often available for those who plan ahead.

Use the Swiss Travel Pass

The Swiss Travel Pass offers unlimited travel on the Swiss Travel System network, which includes trains, buses, and boats. It also provides free or discounted entry to many attractions and museums. This pass can be a cost-effective option if you plan to explore beyond Zermatt.

Opt for Budget Accommodation
Consider staying in budget accommodations such as hostels, guesthouses, or vacation rentals. These options are often more affordable than hotels and can provide a comfortable stay. Websites like Airbnb and Booking.com offer a range of budget-friendly options.

Self-Cater Meals
Eating out in Zermatt can be expensive, so consider self-catering some of your meals. Many accommodations offer kitchen facilities, allowing you to prepare your own food. Grocery stores like Coop and Migros provide a wide range of affordable groceries.

Look for Package Deals

Many travel agencies and online booking platforms offer package deals that combine accommodation, transportation, and activities at a discounted rate. These packages can provide significant savings compared to booking each component separately.

Take Advantage of Free Activities

Zermatt offers numerous free activities, especially for nature lovers. Hiking, sightseeing, and exploring the charming village don't cost anything and can be incredibly rewarding. Additionally, many hotels offer complimentary perks such as shuttle services and guided tours.

Travel with a Group

Traveling with a group can help reduce costs through shared expenses. Group rates for activities, accommodations, and transportation are often available, making it more affordable per person.

Use Discount Cards

Consider purchasing discount cards like the Swiss Half Fare Card, which provides a 50% discount on most trains, buses, and boats throughout Switzerland. This card can significantly reduce your transportation costs.

Affordable Accommodation and Dining Options

Finding affordable accommodation and dining options in Zermatt is key to staying within your budget while enjoying all that this picturesque destination has to offer.

Budget Accommodation Options

- Hostels: Hostels are a popular choice for budget travelers. The Zermatt Youth Hostel offers dormitory beds starting at around CHF 40 per night, including breakfast. Hostels provide a social atmosphere and basic amenities at an affordable price.
- Guesthouses: Guesthouses and B&Bs offer a more personal touch compared to hotels. Places like the Hotel Helvetia and the Matterhorn Hostel provide comfortable rooms at reasonable rates, typically ranging from CHF 50-100 per night.
- Vacation Rentals: Platforms like Airbnb offer a variety of vacation rentals, from private rooms to entire apartments. Renting an apartment with a kitchen can save money on meals, and prices vary widely based on location and amenities.
- Campgrounds: For those who enjoy the outdoors, camping is an affordable option. The nearby Täsch campsite provides pitches

for tents and caravans, with prices starting at around CHF 20 per night.

Affordable Dining Options

- Supermarkets: Grocery stores like Coop and Migros offer a wide selection of fresh produce, ready-made meals, and snacks. Preparing your own meals can significantly cut down on dining expenses.
- Bakeries and Cafes: Local bakeries and cafes offer delicious and affordable options for breakfast and lunch. Places like Biner Bakery and Fuchs Bakery are known for their pastries, sandwiches, and coffee.
- Pizzerias and Fast Food: Zermatt has several pizzerias and fast food outlets that provide tasty meals at reasonable prices. Pizzeria Molino and McDonald's are popular choices for budget-friendly dining.
- Self-Service Restaurants: Many mountain huts and ski resorts have self-service

restaurants that offer hearty meals at lower prices than sit-down restaurants. The Zermatt Bergrestaurant at Sunnegga is one such place where you can enjoy a meal with a view without breaking the bank.

Ethnic Cuisine: Ethnic restaurants often offer good value for money. Zermatt has several Asian, Indian, and Middle Eastern restaurants that provide affordable dining options. Little China and Indian Village are notable examples.

Budgeting for a trip to Zermatt involves careful estimation of costs, smart saving strategies, and finding affordable accommodation and dining options. By planning ahead and making informed choices, you can enjoy all that Zermatt has to offer without exceeding your budget. Whether you're seeking adventure on the slopes, exploring hiking trails, or simply soaking in the breathtaking views, a well-budgeted trip ensures a memorable and enjoyable experience in this alpine paradise.

Chapter 5: Essentials for Traveling

Packing List

Packing for a trip to Zermatt requires thoughtful preparation due to the town's alpine climate and diverse range of activities. Here's a comprehensive packing list to ensure you have everything you need:

Clothing

- Layers: Zermatt's weather can change quickly, so pack multiple layers to stay comfortable. Include base layers, mid-layers (like fleece or sweaters), and a waterproof and windproof outer layer.
- Winter Gear: If visiting in winter, pack thermal underwear, insulated ski or snowboarding pants, a waterproof ski jacket,

and wool socks. Don't forget a warm hat, gloves, and a neck gaiter or scarf.
- Summer Gear: For summer trips, bring lightweight, breathable clothing, but also include warmer items for cool evenings. Pack hiking pants, shorts, t-shirts, a lightweight jacket, and a hat for sun protection.
- Footwear: Sturdy, waterproof hiking boots are essential for exploring trails. Bring comfortable walking shoes for around town and warm, insulated boots for winter visits.
- Swimwear: Many hotels and spas in Zermatt have pools and wellness facilities, so pack a swimsuit if you plan to take advantage of these amenities.

Outdoor Equipment

- Ski/Snowboard Gear: If you plan to ski or snowboard, you can either bring your own equipment or rent it in Zermatt. Essential items include skis or a snowboard, poles, boots, helmet, and goggles.

- Hiking Gear: A good quality backpack, hiking poles, and a hydration system are crucial for long hikes. Don't forget a map, compass or GPS device, and a small first aid kit.
- Climbing Gear: If you're planning to climb, bring appropriate gear such as a climbing harness, ropes, carabiners, and a helmet. Guided tours usually provide equipment, but check in advance.

Personal Items

- Travel Documents: Carry your passport, visas (if required), travel insurance details, and any booking confirmations. It's wise to have both physical copies and digital backups.
- Money and Cards: Bring a mix of cash (Swiss Francs) and credit/debit cards. ATMs are available in Zermatt, but it's good to have cash for small purchases.

- Electronics: A camera, smartphone, chargers, and power banks are essential. Don't forget a power adapter if you're coming from a country with a different plug type.
- Toiletries: Include basic toiletries such as toothpaste, toothbrush, shampoo, conditioner, and personal medications. High SPF sunscreen and lip balm are crucial due to the high altitude.

Miscellaneous

- Sunglasses: High UV protection sunglasses are necessary to protect your eyes from the strong alpine sun.
- Reusable Water Bottle: Staying hydrated is essential, especially at high altitudes. A reusable water bottle helps reduce plastic waste.

- Snacks: Energy bars, nuts, and dried fruits are good to have on hand for quick snacks during activities.

Health and Safety Tips

Ensuring your health and safety during your trip to Zermatt is paramount. Here are some key tips:

Altitude Awareness

- Acclimatization: Zermatt sits at an altitude of about 1,620 meters (5,315 feet). If you're coming from a lower altitude, allow yourself time to acclimate to avoid altitude sickness. Symptoms include headaches, nausea, and dizziness.
- Hydration: Drink plenty of water to stay hydrated, as altitude can cause dehydration more quickly.

- Pacing: Take it easy during your first few days. Avoid strenuous activities until you feel fully acclimated.

Weather Preparedness

- Check Forecasts: Regularly check weather forecasts and be prepared for sudden changes. Zermatt's weather can be unpredictable, especially in the mountains.
- Emergency Supplies: Carry a basic first aid kit, a multi-tool, and a flashlight. In winter, avalanche safety equipment (beacon, probe, and shovel) is essential if venturing off-piste.

Activity Safety

- Guided Tours: For skiing, snowboarding, or climbing, consider hiring a guide. They can provide valuable local knowledge and ensure your safety.

- Trail Conditions: Stay informed about trail conditions for hiking and climbing. Some trails may be closed due to weather or maintenance.

Health Precautions

- Vaccinations: Ensure you're up to date on routine vaccinations. Check if any additional vaccinations are recommended for Switzerland.
- Medical Kit: Bring a basic medical kit with pain relievers, antiseptic, bandages, and any prescription medications.
- Local Healthcare: Familiarize yourself with the locations of medical facilities in Zermatt. The town has a medical center that can handle emergencies.

Travel Insurance

Travel insurance is a critical aspect of trip planning, offering financial protection and peace of mind. Here's why it's essential and what to look for in a good policy:

Why You Need Travel Insurance

- Medical Emergencies: Health care costs in Switzerland can be high. Travel insurance covers medical expenses, including hospital stays, doctor visits, and emergency evacuations.
- Trip Cancellation: If unforeseen circumstances force you to cancel your trip, travel insurance can reimburse non-refundable expenses such as flights and accommodations.
- Lost or Stolen Belongings: Travel insurance can cover the cost of lost, stolen, or damaged luggage and personal items.
- Activity Coverage: Zermatt offers many outdoor activities, some of which can be

risky. Ensure your policy covers activities like skiing, snowboarding, and mountaineering.

Choosing the Right Policy

- Coverage Limits: Look for a policy with high coverage limits for medical expenses, emergency evacuation, and trip cancellation.
- Activity Inclusions: Make sure the policy includes coverage for all the activities you plan to undertake. Some standard policies may not cover high-risk activities.
- Pre-existing Conditions: Check if the policy covers pre-existing medical conditions. Some insurers offer this coverage if you purchase the policy within a specific timeframe.
- Travel Assistance Services: Many policies include 24/7 travel assistance services to help with emergencies, such as locating medical facilities or arranging evacuations.

Additional Considerations

- Policy Duration: Ensure your travel insurance covers the entire duration of your trip. Some policies offer annual coverage if you travel frequently.
- Read the Fine Print: Understand the terms and conditions, including any exclusions or limitations. Knowing what is and isn't covered can prevent surprises later.
- Compare Providers: Shop around and compare policies from different providers. Online comparison tools can help you find the best coverage at a competitive price.

How to Use Travel Insurance

- Emergency Contacts: Keep a copy of your insurance policy and emergency contact numbers with you at all times.
- Document Everything: In case of a claim, document all incidents thoroughly. Keep

receipts, medical reports, and any other relevant documentation.
- Contact the Insurer Promptly: In an emergency, contact your insurance provider as soon as possible. They can guide you through the process and ensure you receive the necessary assistance.

Preparing for a trip to Zermatt involves thoughtful packing, staying aware of health and safety considerations, and securing comprehensive travel insurance. By following these guidelines, you can ensure a smooth and enjoyable journey, fully equipped to handle any challenges that may arise. Whether you're hitting the slopes, hiking the trails, or simply soaking in the stunning alpine scenery, being well-prepared will help you make the most of your Zermatt adventure.

Chapter 6: Entry and Visa Requirements

Visa Information for Different Nationalities

When planning a trip to Zermatt, it's essential to understand Switzerland's entry and visa requirements. These requirements vary depending on your nationality, the purpose of your visit, and the duration of your stay.

Citizens of the European Union (EU) and European Free Trade Association (EFTA)

Citizens of EU and EFTA countries (Iceland, Liechtenstein, Norway, and Switzerland) do not require a visa to enter Switzerland. They can stay in the country for up to 90 days within a 180-day period for tourism, business, or visiting family and friends. Travelers must carry a valid passport or national identity card.

Citizens of the Schengen Area

Switzerland is part of the Schengen Area, which comprises 26 European countries that have abolished passport controls at their mutual borders. Citizens of Schengen Area countries can travel to Switzerland without a visa for up to 90 days within a 180-day period. They must carry a valid passport or national identity card.

Citizens of Visa-Exempt Countries

Citizens of several countries, including the United States, Canada, Australia, New Zealand, Japan, South Korea, and Singapore, do not need a visa to enter Switzerland for stays of up to 90 days within a 180-day period. Travelers must have a passport valid for at least three months beyond their intended departure date from the Schengen Area.

Citizens of Non-Visa-Exempt Countries

Citizens of countries not listed as visa-exempt must obtain a Schengen visa to enter Switzerland. This visa allows travel within the Schengen Area for up to 90 days within a 180-day period. The application process involves submitting a completed application form, a valid passport, recent passport-sized photos, travel itinerary, proof of accommodation, travel insurance, and proof of financial means. The application must be submitted at the Swiss embassy or consulate in the applicant's home country. Processing times can vary, so it's advisable to apply well in advance of your planned travel dates.

Long-Stay Visas

For those intending to stay in Switzerland for more than 90 days, such as for work, study, or family reunification, a long-stay visa (D visa) is required. The application process for a long-stay visa is more comprehensive and includes additional documentation, such as proof of employment or enrollment in an educational institution. The application must be submitted to the Swiss embassy or consulate in your home country.

Customs Regulations

Switzerland has specific customs regulations that travelers should be aware of to avoid any issues upon entry. Here are some key points regarding customs regulations:

Personal Effects

Travelers can bring personal effects, such as clothing, toiletries, and electronic devices, into Switzerland without paying customs duties. These items must be for personal use and not intended for sale.

Alcohol and Tobacco

Travelers aged 17 and older are allowed to bring the following quantities of alcohol and tobacco

products into Switzerland without paying customs duties:
- Alcohol: Up to 1 liter of spirits (over 18% alcohol) and up to 4 liters of wine or beer (under 18% alcohol).
- Tobacco: Up to 200 cigarettes, 50 cigars, or 250 grams of other tobacco products.

Amounts exceeding these limits are subject to customs duties and taxes.

Food and Animal Products

Travelers are allowed to bring small quantities of food and non-meat animal products for personal use into Switzerland. However, there are restrictions on meat and meat products, dairy products, and certain plants and plant products to prevent the spread of diseases and pests. It's advisable to check the specific regulations if you plan to bring such items.

Cash and Monetary Instruments

Travelers carrying more than CHF 10,000 (or equivalent in other currencies) in cash or monetary instruments must declare it to Swiss customs. Failure to declare can result in penalties and confiscation of the undeclared amount.

Prohibited and Restricted Items

Certain items are prohibited or restricted from being brought into Switzerland. These include:
- Weapons and Ammunition: Strict regulations apply to the import of firearms, ammunition, and other weapons. Import permits are required.
- Endangered Species: Importing products made from endangered species, such as ivory and certain animal skins, is prohibited under the Convention on International Trade in Endangered Species (CITES).
- Illegal Drugs: The import, possession, and use of illegal drugs are strictly prohibited and subject to severe penalties.

- Counterfeit Goods: Importing counterfeit goods, such as fake designer products, is illegal and can result in fines and confiscation of the items.

Important Travel Documents

To ensure a smooth entry into Switzerland and enjoy your stay in Zermatt, it's crucial to have all the necessary travel documents. Here's a checklist of essential documents:

Passport

A valid passport is required for entry into Switzerland. Ensure that your passport is valid for at least three months beyond your intended departure date from the Schengen Area. For some nationalities, this requirement may vary, so it's best to check the specific regulations for your country.

Visa

If you require a visa to enter Switzerland, ensure that it is valid for the duration of your stay. Carry a copy of your visa approval letter and any supporting documents you submitted during the application process.

Travel Insurance

Travel insurance is highly recommended for all travelers to Switzerland. It should cover medical expenses, emergency evacuation, trip cancellation, and loss or theft of belongings. Carry a copy of your travel insurance policy and the emergency contact numbers of your insurance provider.

Proof of Accommodation

Be prepared to provide proof of accommodation for the duration of your stay in Switzerland. This can be in the form of hotel reservations, rental agreements, or an invitation letter from a host.

Return or Onward Travel Ticket

Swiss authorities may require proof of a return or onward travel ticket to ensure that you intend to leave the country within the allowed period. Keep a copy of your flight or train tickets readily available.

Financial Proof

You may be asked to provide proof of sufficient funds to cover your expenses during your stay in Switzerland. This can include bank statements, credit card statements, or a letter from a sponsor.

Travel Itinerary

Having a detailed travel itinerary can be helpful, especially if you're applying for a visa. It should include your planned activities, accommodation details, and transportation arrangements.

Health Documents

Depending on your country of origin and recent travel history, you may need to provide health documents such as vaccination records or a negative COVID-19 test result. Check the latest health and entry requirements before your trip.

Emergency Contacts

Carry a list of emergency contacts, including family members, your country's embassy or consulate in Switzerland, and local emergency services.

Copies of Important Documents

Make copies of all important documents, including your passport, visa, travel insurance policy, and accommodation details. Store these copies separately from the originals in case of loss or theft. Digital copies stored securely on your smartphone or cloud storage can also be helpful.

Language Translation

If you don't speak the local languages (German, French, Italian), having important documents translated or having a translation app can be useful. This includes your travel insurance policy, medical records, and other critical documents.

Understanding entry and visa requirements, customs regulations, and important travel documents is crucial for a hassle-free trip to Zermatt. By ensuring you have the necessary documents and are aware of the customs regulations, you can focus on enjoying the breathtaking scenery and activities that Zermatt has to offer. Planning ahead and being well-prepared will help you make the most of your visit to this stunning alpine destination.

Chapter 7: Getting to Zermatt

Transportation Options

Zermatt, a picturesque village nestled at the foot of the Matterhorn, is renowned for its stunning alpine scenery and excellent skiing. Getting to Zermatt involves a journey through some of Switzerland's most beautiful landscapes, with various transportation options available.

By Air

The closest international airports to Zermatt are Zurich Airport (ZRH), Geneva Airport (GVA), and Milan Malpensa Airport (MXP) in Italy. These airports are well-connected with major cities worldwide and offer a range of services to ensure a smooth travel experience.

- Zurich Airport: Located about 250 kilometers from Zermatt, Zurich Airport is Switzerland's largest and busiest airport. From Zurich, travelers can take a direct train to Zermatt, which takes approximately 3.5 hours.
- Geneva Airport: Situated approximately 230 kilometers from Zermatt, Geneva Airport is another major gateway. The train journey from Geneva to Zermatt also takes around 3.5 hours with direct and connecting options.
- Milan Malpensa Airport: Located about 185 kilometers from Zermatt, Milan Malpensa offers another route, especially for travelers coming from Italy. The train journey from

Milan to Zermatt, via Domodossola, takes around 4 hours.

By Train

Switzerland's efficient and scenic train network makes train travel a popular option for reaching Zermatt. The Swiss Federal Railways (SBB) operates frequent and reliable services. Key routes include:

- From Zurich: Direct trains from Zurich to Zermatt run several times a day, taking about 3.5 hours.
- From Geneva: Trains from Geneva to Zermatt, with both direct and connecting services via Visp, also take about 3.5 hours.
- From Milan: The journey from Milan to Zermatt involves a train to Domodossola and then a connection to Zermatt, taking around 4 hours.

By Car

While Zermatt itself is car-free, driving to nearby
Täsch is an option. Täsch, located 5 kilometers from
Zermatt, serves as the gateway for those arriving by
car. Secure parking facilities are available in Täsch,
and from there, travelers can take a shuttle train or
taxi to Zermatt, which takes about 12 minutes.

By Shuttle Services
Various private shuttle services operate between
major airports and Zermatt. These services provide
a convenient and comfortable option, especially for
travelers with heavy luggage or in groups. Shuttle
buses can be pre-booked and offer door-to-door
service, although they can be more expensive than
trains.

Navigating Airports and Train Stations

Navigating through airports and train stations in
Switzerland is generally straightforward due to

excellent signage and organization. Here's what you
need to know:

Airports
- Zurich Airport (ZRH): Zurich Airport is well-organized, with clear signage in multiple languages. Upon arrival, follow the signs for customs and baggage claim. The airport has a direct connection to the train station, located below the terminal. Purchase train tickets at the SBB counters or ticket machines.
- Geneva Airport (GVA): Geneva Airport is similarly well-signposted. After collecting your luggage, follow the signs to the train station, which is connected to the airport. Tickets can be purchased at the SBB counters or from machines.
- Milan Malpensa Airport (MXP): In Milan, follow the signs for trains to reach the Malpensa Express, which connects to central

Milan. From there, you can catch a train to Domodossola and onward to Zermatt.

Train Stations

- Zurich Hauptbahnhof (HB): Zurich's main train station is one of Europe's busiest, but it is well-organized with clear signs and multiple platforms. Information boards display train schedules, and SBB staff are available to assist.
- Geneva Cornavin: Geneva's main station is also centrally located with excellent facilities. Information desks and automated ticket machines are readily available.
- Visp: For those traveling to Zermatt, Visp is a key transfer point. The station is smaller but well-signposted, making it easy to navigate for transferring trains.

Purchasing Tickets

- Online: Train tickets can be purchased online through the SBB website or app, which is convenient and allows you to reserve seats.
- At Stations: Tickets can also be bought at ticket counters or machines at all major stations and airports. Machines usually accept major credit cards and multiple currencies.

Local Transportation in Zermatt

Zermatt is a car-free village, which enhances its charm and environmental sustainability. Here's how you can navigate locally:

Electric Taxis

Electric taxis are a popular mode of transport within Zermatt. These small, eco-friendly vehicles can be hired to transport you and your luggage from the train station to your accommodation. They are particularly useful if you have heavy bags or are staying at a location far from the train station.

E-Buses

Zermatt operates a network of e-buses that run regularly throughout the village. These buses are convenient for getting around and reaching various parts of Zermatt, including the ski lifts and major hotels. The buses are quiet and non-polluting, making them a great option for local travel.

Hotel Shuttles

Many hotels in Zermatt offer complimentary shuttle services to and from the train station. Check with your accommodation provider if this service is available and arrange for pickup if necessary. This can be a hassle-free way to reach your hotel, especially if you have a lot of luggage.

Walking

Zermatt is a compact village, and many places of
interest are within walking distance. Walking is
often the best way to explore Zermatt, allowing you
to soak in the stunning alpine views and charming
streets. The village has well-maintained paths and
signage, making it easy to navigate on foot.

Bicycle Rentals

For those who prefer cycling, Zermatt offers bicycle
rentals, including electric bikes. Renting a bike can
be an enjoyable way to explore the area and cover
more ground quickly. There are various rental
shops in the village, and electric bikes make it
easier to handle the hilly terrain.

Gornergrat Railway

One of Zermatt's highlights is the Gornergrat
Railway, a cogwheel train that takes you from the
village to the Gornergrat summit. This scenic ride
offers breathtaking views of the Matterhorn and
surrounding peaks. The train runs year-round and
is a must-do for visitors.

Sunnegga Funicular

The Sunnegga funicular is another key transport option, taking you from Zermatt up to the Sunnegga paradise, a popular starting point for skiing and hiking. The funicular operates regularly and is an efficient way to reach the higher elevations quickly.

Cable Cars and Gondolas

Zermatt has an extensive network of cable cars and gondolas that connect the village to the ski slopes and hiking trails. These lifts are modern and provide easy access to various mountain areas, including the Matterhorn Glacier Paradise, Rothorn, and Schwarzsee.

Tips for Using Local Transportation

- Timetables: Check the timetables for buses, funiculars, and cable cars in advance. They are usually available online or at your hotel.
- Tickets: Purchase tickets for electric taxis, e-buses, and other local transport modes at

- designated points or through apps. Multi-day passes can offer savings if you plan to use public transport frequently.
- Seasonal Variations: Be aware that schedules for some transport options may vary between summer and winter seasons. Always check for the latest information, especially if you are visiting during the shoulder seasons.

Getting to Zermatt involves a combination of air, train, and local transportation options, each offering a unique travel experience through Switzerland's scenic landscapes. Navigating airports and train stations is straightforward thanks to excellent infrastructure and clear signage, while local transportation within Zermatt is eco-friendly and convenient, ensuring you can explore the village and its stunning surroundings with ease. Proper planning and understanding of the available transport options will ensure a smooth and enjoyable journey to this alpine paradise.

Chapter 8: Accommodation in Zermatt

Types of Accommodation

Zermatt offers a wide range of accommodation options to suit different budgets and preferences. From luxury hotels to cozy chalets and budget-friendly hostels, there's something for everyone. Here's a breakdown of the types of accommodation you can find in Zermatt:

Luxury Hotels

Zermatt is home to several luxury hotels that offer world-class amenities and services. These hotels often feature stunning views of the Matterhorn, gourmet dining options, spa facilities, and top-notch customer service. Examples include:

- The Omnia: Known for its modern design and exceptional service, The Omnia offers

luxurious rooms and suites, an indoor pool, and a wellness area.
- Mont Cervin Palace: This historic hotel provides elegant rooms, multiple dining options, and a comprehensive spa.
- Hotel Zermatterhof: Offering a blend of tradition and luxury, this hotel features beautifully appointed rooms, fine dining, and wellness facilities.

Mid-Range Hotels

For those seeking comfort without the high price tag, Zermatt has a variety of mid-range hotels. These hotels provide good value for money with comfortable rooms and essential amenities.

- Hotel Bellerive: A family-run hotel offering stylish rooms, a cozy atmosphere, and a wellness area with a sauna and hot tub.
- Hotel La Couronne: Known for its friendly service and comfortable rooms, this hotel

also offers a convenient location close to the ski lifts.
- Hotel Sonne: Featuring modern rooms and a wellness area, Hotel Sonne is a great option for those looking for comfort and convenience.

Chalets and Apartments

For a more home-like experience, renting a chalet or apartment can be an excellent choice. This option is particularly popular among families and groups who want more space and the ability to cook their own meals.

- Chalet Zermatt Peak: A luxurious chalet with stunning views, offering five bedrooms, a private spa, and concierge services.
- Haus Mischabel: Comfortable and well-equipped apartments located close to the village center and ski lifts.

- Haus Alpenglühn: Offering spacious apartments with modern amenities, Haus Alpenglühn is ideal for longer stays.

Budget Accommodation

Zermatt also caters to budget-conscious travelers with hostels and budget hotels that provide basic but comfortable lodging.

- Zermatt Youth Hostel: Offering dormitory and private rooms, this hostel is a great option for backpackers and budget travelers. It also includes a restaurant and common areas.
- Matterhorn Hostel: Located close to the ski lifts, this hostel offers affordable accommodation with shared facilities.
- Hotel Bahnhof: A budget-friendly hotel with simple rooms, located conveniently near the train station.

Choosing the Right Area

Selecting the right area to stay in Zermatt depends on your preferences and planned activities. Here are some considerations to help you choose the best area for your stay:

Village Center

Staying in the village center puts you close to the main amenities, including shops, restaurants, and bars. It's a great option for those who want to be in the heart of the action and enjoy easy access to everything Zermatt has to offer.

- Pros: Proximity to amenities, lively atmosphere, and convenient access to public transport and ski lifts.
- Cons: Can be busy and noisy, especially during peak seasons.

Near the Ski Lifts

If skiing or snowboarding is your main focus, consider staying near the ski lifts. This area offers the convenience of quick access to the slopes, minimizing the time spent commuting.

- Pros: Immediate access to ski lifts, ski-in/ski-out options, and reduced travel time to the slopes.
- Cons: Accommodation in this area can be more expensive, and dining options might be limited.

Hinterdorf

Hinterdorf is the historic part of Zermatt, known for its traditional wooden houses and charming atmosphere. Staying here offers a more tranquil experience while still being close to the village center.

- Pros: Quaint, peaceful surroundings with traditional architecture and close proximity to the center.
- Cons: Limited modern amenities and fewer accommodation options.

Winkelmatten

Located slightly away from the village center, Winkelmatten is a quieter residential area with stunning views of the Matterhorn. It's ideal for those looking for a more serene environment.

- Pros: Peaceful, scenic views, and family-friendly environment with parks and playgrounds.
- Cons: Slightly longer walk or shuttle ride to the village center and ski lifts.

Near the Train Station

For convenience, especially if you're arriving with a
lot of luggage, staying near the train station can be a
good choice. This area offers easy access to
transport links and is still close to the main
attractions.

- Pros: Convenient for arrival and departure, close to public transport, and easy access to the village center.
- Cons: Less picturesque than other areas and can be noisier due to train activity.

Booking Tips

To ensure you get the best accommodation for your
needs and budget, consider the following booking
tips:

Book Early

Zermatt is a popular destination, especially during peak seasons (winter for skiing and summer for hiking). Booking your accommodation early ensures better availability and often better rates. Aim to book at least 6-12 months in advance for peak periods.

Compare Prices

Use online booking platforms such as Booking.com, Expedia, and Airbnb to compare prices and read reviews. These platforms often offer discounts and special deals, so it's worth checking multiple sites before making a reservation.

Consider Packages

Some hotels and chalets offer package deals that include lift passes, equipment rental, or dining options. These packages can provide good value and simplify planning, especially for first-time visitors.

Flexible Dates

If your travel dates are flexible, you might find better rates during shoulder seasons (late spring and early autumn). Mid-week stays can also be cheaper than weekends, so consider adjusting your schedule to save money.

Check Cancellation Policies

Ensure you understand the cancellation policy before booking. Some accommodations offer free cancellation up to a certain date, providing flexibility if your plans change. This can be particularly important in times of uncertainty, such as during a pandemic.

Look for Amenities

Identify which amenities are important to you, such as Wi-Fi, breakfast, spa facilities, or proximity to ski lifts. Filter your search results based on these preferences to find accommodation that best suits your needs.

Contact the Property Directly

Sometimes contacting the hotel or rental property directly can result in better rates or additional perks, such as free breakfast or room upgrades. It's worth sending an email or making a phone call to inquire about any potential offers.

Read Reviews

Reading guest reviews can provide valuable insights into the quality of the accommodation and the experiences of previous visitors. Pay attention to recent reviews and look for consistent feedback on cleanliness, service, and location.

Consider Local Recommendations

Local tourism websites and travel forums can offer recommendations for accommodation that may not be widely advertised. These sources can provide unique options that add to the authenticity of your Zermatt experience.

Zermatt offers a wide variety of accommodation options to suit all budgets and preferences.

Whether you're looking for luxury, mid-range comfort, or budget-friendly options, planning ahead and considering the right area for your stay will help ensure a memorable and enjoyable visit to this beautiful alpine destination.

Chapter 9: Cultural Experiences

Local Traditions and Festivals

Zermatt, nestled in the Swiss Alps, is a town steeped in rich traditions and vibrant festivals that reflect its cultural heritage and alpine lifestyle. One of the most notable traditions is the **Zermatt Unplugged Festival**, which takes place every April. This unique music festival features acoustic performances by renowned international artists in intimate settings, including mountain huts and open-air stages. The event draws music lovers from around the world and showcases Zermatt's ability to blend modern entertainment with its rustic charm.

Another significant tradition is the **Zermatt Folklore Festival**, held every August. This festival

is a celebration of Swiss heritage, with locals
dressed in traditional costumes, performing folk
dances, and playing alpine instruments like the
alphorn. The streets of Zermatt come alive with
colorful parades, yodeling competitions, and craft
markets, offering visitors a glimpse into the town's
cultural roots and community spirit.

Winter in Zermatt brings the **Christmas
Market**, a festive tradition that transforms the
town into a winter wonderland. Stalls selling
handcrafted gifts, local delicacies, and mulled wine
line the streets, while the aroma of roasted
chestnuts fills the air. The highlight is the
Christmas Eve torchlight descent, where skiers
glide down the slopes with torches, creating a
magical spectacle against the snowy backdrop.

The **Shepherd Festival**, held in mid-September,
is another unique event that reflects Zermatt's
pastoral traditions. During this festival, local
shepherds bring their sheep down from the summer

pastures, parading them through the town. It's a time of celebration with traditional music, dancing, and feasting, emphasizing the close-knit relationship between the community and its agrarian roots.

Zermatt also celebrates Swiss National Day on August 1st with great enthusiasm. The day begins with a parade featuring local clubs and associations, followed by speeches, concerts, and fireworks. The festivities reflect a deep sense of national pride and community cohesion, offering visitors a chance to experience Swiss patriotism firsthand.

The town's traditions extend to the culinary realm as well, with events like the **Raclette Festival**, celebrating one of Switzerland's most famous dishes. During this festival, local restaurants and stalls serve raclette cheese melted over potatoes, accompanied by pickles and onions. It's a communal experience that brings people together to enjoy this beloved Swiss specialty.

Zermatt's festivals and traditions are not just events but a reflection of the town's identity and heritage. They offer visitors a chance to connect with the local culture, participate in time-honored customs, and experience the warmth and hospitality of the Zermatt community. Whether it's through music, dance, food, or seasonal celebrations, Zermatt's traditions provide a rich cultural tapestry that enhances the travel experience and leaves lasting memories.

Cuisine and Dining Experiences

Zermatt's culinary scene is a delightful blend of traditional Swiss flavors and innovative gourmet cuisine, reflecting the town's diverse cultural influences and alpine heritage. The town offers a range of dining experiences, from rustic mountain huts serving hearty local dishes to Michelin-starred restaurants offering refined gastronomic delights.

One of the quintessential Zermatt dining experiences is enjoying **raclette** or **fondue** in a cozy mountain hut. Raclette involves melting a wheel of cheese and scraping it over boiled potatoes, pickles, and onions, while fondue features a communal pot of melted cheese in which diners dip pieces of bread. Restaurants like **Chez Vrony** and **Findlerhof** provide these traditional dishes with stunning views of the Matterhorn, creating a perfect alpine dining experience.

For those seeking gourmet cuisine, **The Omnia** and **After Seven** offer exceptional dining experiences. These Michelin-starred restaurants emphasize local ingredients and innovative cooking techniques, creating dishes that are both visually stunning and exquisitely flavored. The chefs here often draw inspiration from the surrounding alpine environment, incorporating regional ingredients such as wild game, fresh mountain herbs, and locally sourced dairy products.

Zermatt's culinary scene also embraces international flavors, reflecting its global appeal. Restaurants like **Cervo Puro** offer a fusion of Swiss and Mediterranean cuisine, featuring dishes such as truffle pasta and seafood risotto alongside traditional Swiss fare. This blend of flavors caters to a wide range of palates, ensuring that every visitor finds something to savor.

In addition to its restaurants, Zermatt is home to several mountain huts and on-piste dining options that provide a unique alpine experience. **Fluhalp** and **Riffelalp Resort** offer hearty meals and refreshments in a picturesque setting, perfect for skiers and hikers looking to refuel while enjoying panoramic mountain views. These establishments often serve traditional dishes such as **alp macaroni** (a Swiss version of macaroni and cheese with potatoes and onions) and **rosti** (a crispy potato dish), providing a taste of local cuisine in a casual, relaxed atmosphere.

Zermatt's vibrant food scene extends to its bustling farmers' markets and specialty food shops. The weekly market is a treasure trove of local produce, artisanal cheeses, cured meats, and freshly baked bread. **Läderach** and **Fuchs** are renowned for their Swiss chocolates and pastries, offering sweet treats that are perfect souvenirs of your trip.

For wine enthusiasts, Zermatt boasts a selection of fine Swiss wines, particularly those from the nearby Valais region. Wine bars like **Alpine Gourmet Prato Borni** and **Grampis Pub** offer curated selections of local wines, allowing visitors to sample varietals such as Fendant, Pinot Noir, and Petite Arvine. These establishments often provide cozy, intimate settings for wine tasting, enhancing the overall dining experience.

In summary, Zermatt's culinary landscape is a rich tapestry of traditional Swiss dishes, international cuisine, and gourmet innovations. Whether dining in a rustic hut or a Michelin-starred restaurant, visitors are treated to an array of flavors that reflect the town's cultural diversity and alpine heritage. The focus on high-quality, locally sourced ingredients and the variety of dining settings—from casual mountain huts to elegant dining rooms—ensure that every meal in Zermatt is a memorable part of the Swiss Alps adventure.

Museums and Historical Sites

Zermatt's museums and historical sites offer a fascinating glimpse into the town's rich heritage, alpine culture, and the adventurous spirit of its people. These cultural institutions and landmarks provide valuable insights into Zermatt's development from a remote mountain village to a world-renowned tourist destination.

The **Matterhorn Museum – Zermatlantis** is the centerpiece of Zermatt's cultural offerings. Located in the heart of the town, this museum is an underground treasure trove that vividly brings Zermatt's history to life. The museum's exhibits are housed in a reconstructed alpine village, complete with traditional chalets, workshops, and stores. Visitors can explore the history of mountaineering in the region, with a special focus on the first successful ascent of the Matterhorn in 1865 by Edward Whymper. The museum showcases original equipment, photographs, and personal items of the climbers, offering a poignant narrative of their triumphs and tragedies. Interactive displays and multimedia presentations make the history engaging and accessible to all ages.

Another significant historical site is the Mountaineers' Cemetery, located near St. Mauritius Church. This serene and poignant cemetery is the final resting place of many climbers who lost their lives attempting to conquer the Matterhorn and other surrounding peaks. Each gravestone tells a story of adventure, bravery, and sometimes tragedy, serving as a solemn reminder of the challenges posed by the mighty Alps. The cemetery is a place of reflection and respect, honoring the memory of those who pursued their passion for mountaineering.

St. Mauritius Church itself is a historical landmark worth visiting. This Roman Catholic church, with its distinctive pointed spire, has been a spiritual center for the Zermatt community for centuries. Inside, visitors can admire beautiful stained-glass windows and intricate woodwork, reflecting the town's religious heritage and artistic craftsmanship. The adjacent English Church, built in the 19th century to serve the growing number of British visitors, is another architectural gem that adds to Zermatt's historical tapestry.

For a unique cultural experience, the **Gornergrat Railway** offers more than just stunning views. This historic cogwheel railway, inaugurated in 1898, was the world's first fully electrified cog railway. The journey to the Gornergrat summit provides breathtaking panoramas of the Matterhorn and surrounding peaks, but it also tells the story of technological innovation and the development of tourism in the Swiss Alps. The railway stations and the Gornergrat Kulm Hotel, with its observatory and panoramic restaurant, are historical sites in their own right, showcasing the blend of natural beauty and human ingenuity.

Zermatt's rich history is also reflected in its traditional alpine architecture. Walking through the old village, visitors can see well-preserved **Valaisan wooden houses**, barns, and granaries, some of which date back several centuries. These buildings, made from larch wood and set on stilts to protect against rodents and moisture, offer a window into the past and the traditional ways of life in this alpine region.

The **Alpine Museum** in nearby Täsch is another important cultural site, providing further context on the region's natural and cultural history. The museum features exhibits on the geology, flora, and fauna of the Alps, as well as the daily life and customs of the local people. It's an excellent complement to the Matterhorn Museum, providing a broader understanding of the alpine environment and its influence on the local culture.

Zermatt's museums and historical sites are integral to understanding the town's unique cultural heritage and the adventurous spirit of its inhabitants. From the captivating exhibits at the

Matterhorn Museum to the poignant Mountaineers' Cemetery, these sites offer a deep and enriching experience for visitors. They highlight the intersection of natural beauty, human endeavor, and historical development that defines Zermatt, making them essential stops on any comprehensive tour of this iconic alpine destination.

Chapter 10: Accommodation in Zermatt

Luxury Hotels

- Mont Cervin Palace
- Price: CHF 700 - CHF 1500 per night
- Location: Bahnhofstrasse 31, 3920 Zermatt, Switzerland
- Booking Contact: +41 27 966 88 88

Mont Cervin Palace is a historic luxury hotel offering elegance and charm in the heart of Zermatt. With its prime location, guests can enjoy stunning views of the Matterhorn and indulge in world-class amenities including a full-service spa, gourmet dining, and lavish rooms and suites. This hotel is perfect for those seeking a refined and unforgettable stay.

2. The Omnia

- Price: CHF 500 - CHF 1200 per night
- Location: Auf dem Fels, 3920 Zermatt, Switzerland
- Booking Contact: +41 27 966 71 71

Perched on a rock, The Omnia offers a unique blend of contemporary design and natural beauty. This boutique hotel features modern, spacious rooms with panoramic views, an extensive wellness area, and exquisite dining options. The Omnia provides a tranquil retreat while still being conveniently located near Zermatt's main attractions.

3. *Grand Hotel Zermatterhof*

- Price: CHF 600 - CHF 1300 per night
- Location: Bahnhofstrasse 55, 3920 Zermatt, Switzerland
- Booking Contact: +41 27 966 66 00

The Grand Hotel Zermatterhof, with its rich history and traditional alpine charm, offers luxurious accommodations and top-tier services. Guests can enjoy beautifully appointed rooms, an array of dining options, and a comprehensive spa. Its central location makes it a prime choice for travelers looking to explore Zermatt in style.

Budget-Friendly Hotels

1. Hotel Helvetia

- Price: CHF 100 - CHF 200 per night
- Location: Bahnhofstrasse 72, 3920 Zermatt, Switzerland
- Booking Contact: +41 27 967 10 20

Hotel Helvetia offers comfortable accommodations at an affordable price right in the heart of Zermatt. This cozy hotel features simple yet cozy rooms, friendly service, and easy access to the village's shops and restaurants, making it an excellent choice for budget-conscious travelers.

2. Hotel Alfa Zermatt

- Price: CHF 120 - CHF 250 per night
- Location: Obere Mattenstrasse 18, 3920 Zermatt, Switzerland
- Booking Contact: +41 27 966 35 70

Hotel Alfa Zermatt provides budget-friendly lodging with a warm, welcoming atmosphere. Located close to the Zermatt train station and ski lifts, it offers convenience for both winter and summer visitors. Guests can enjoy a complimentary breakfast and basic yet comfortable rooms.

3. Hotel Bahnhof

- Price: CHF 80 - CHF 180 per night
- Location: Bahnhofplatz 54, 3920 Zermatt, Switzerland
- Booking Contact: +41 27 967 24 00

Hotel Bahnhof is perfect for travelers looking for a no-frills, budget-friendly stay. Situated just steps from the train station, this hotel offers clean, basic rooms and a communal kitchen, making it ideal for those looking to save on dining costs. The hotel's location is ideal for exploring Zermatt on foot.

Restaurants in Zermatt

1. Restaurant Chez Vrony

- Location: Findeln, 3920 Zermatt, Switzerland

Restaurant Chez Vrony is renowned for its authentic Swiss cuisine and breathtaking views of the Matterhorn. This family-run restaurant offers a warm, rustic atmosphere and dishes made from locally sourced ingredients. It's a must-visit for anyone looking to experience traditional Swiss dining.

Restaurant Whymper-Stube

- Location: Bahnhofstrasse 80, 3920 Zermatt, Switzerland

Restaurant Whymper-Stube is famous for its delicious fondue and raclette. The cozy, alpine-style restaurant provides a welcoming ambiance and a menu filled with Swiss specialties. It's the perfect place to enjoy a hearty meal after a day of exploring.

3. Restaurant Alpenrose

- Location: Riedweg 5, 3920 Zermatt, Switzerland

Restaurant Alpenrose offers a delightful mix of Swiss and international cuisine. Nestled on a hillside, it provides stunning views of Zermatt and the surrounding mountains. With its friendly service and diverse menu, Alpenrose is a great choice for a relaxed dining experience.

Chapter 11: Five-Day Itinerary for Zermatt

Day 1: Arrival and Exploration

Morning:
- Arrive in Zermatt and check into your hotel.
- Take a leisurely walk around the village to get your bearings.
- Visit the Matterhorn Museum to learn about the history and culture of Zermatt.

Afternoon:
- Enjoy lunch at one of the local cafes.
- Take the Gornergrat Railway up to Gornergrat for spectacular views of the Matterhorn and the surrounding peaks.
- Spend some time exploring the viewing platforms and taking photos.

Evening:

- Dine at Restaurant Whymper-Stube and indulge in traditional Swiss fondue.
- Stroll through the village and enjoy the charming evening ambiance.

Day 2: Skiing and Adventure

Morning:

- Head to the Sunnegga-Rothorn area for a morning of skiing or snowboarding. This area offers slopes suitable for all levels.
- Beginners can take lessons at one of the local ski schools.

Afternoon:

- Have lunch at a mountain restaurant such as Chez Vrony, which offers stunning views and delicious food.

- Continue skiing or try other snow activities like snowshoeing or sledging.

Evening:
- Relax and unwind at your hotel's spa or wellness center.
- Dinner at The Omnia's restaurant, enjoying a gourmet meal with a view.

Day 3: Glacier Paradise and Hiking

Morning:
- Take the cable car to the Klein Matterhorn (Glacier Paradise), the highest cable car station in Europe.
- Explore the ice palace and enjoy panoramic views from the observation deck.

Afternoon:

- Descend to the Trockener Steg station for lunch at the restaurant there.
- Spend the afternoon hiking one of the many trails, such as the hike from Trockener Steg to Schwarzsee.

Evening:
- Dinner at Restaurant Alpenrose, enjoying a mix of Swiss and international cuisine.
- Take a leisurely evening walk along the river.

Day 4: Relaxation and Sightseeing

Morning:
- Sleep in and enjoy a relaxed breakfast at your hotel.
- Visit the Zermatt Bergbahnen (cable car company) and take a ride to the Matterhorn Glacier Paradise.

Afternoon:
- Enjoy lunch at one of the mountaintop restaurants.
- Spend the afternoon at the Riffelsee lake, famous for its reflection of the Matterhorn.

Evening:
- Dinner at your hotel or another local restaurant.
- Visit a local bar or lounge for some evening entertainment and drinks.

Day 5: Departure and Last-minute Exploration

Morning:
- Pack your bags and check out of your hotel.
- Spend the morning doing some last-minute shopping for souvenirs and local products.

Afternoon:

- Have a final lunch at a cafe or restaurant in the village.
- Take a final walk around Zermatt, visiting any sights you may have missed.

Evening:
- Depart from Zermatt, taking with you wonderful memories of your Swiss Alps adventure.

Chapter 12: Outdoor Activities and Attractions

Skiing and Snowboarding

Zermatt is a premier destination for skiing and snowboarding, renowned for its extensive and varied terrain, high altitude, and breathtaking alpine scenery. The resort offers over 360 kilometers of pistes, catering to all skill levels from beginners to advanced skiers and snowboarders. One of the standout features of Zermatt is its snow reliability, with year-round skiing available on the Theodul Glacier. This makes it an ideal destination for winter sports enthusiasts looking for guaranteed snow conditions.

For beginners, the **Sunnegga-Blauherd-Rothorn area** offers gentle slopes and excellent ski schools where newcomers can learn the basics in a supportive environment. Intermediate skiers will find a wealth of blue and red runs across the resort, particularly in the **Gornergrat area**, which provides a mix of scenic routes and more challenging descents.

Advanced skiers and snowboarders are drawn to the **Schwarzsee and Stockhorn areas**, which feature steep, technical runs and off-piste opportunities. The legendary **Zermatt-Cervinia Valtournenche ski area** allows for cross-border skiing into Italy, adding an extra dimension to the skiing experience. This international ski area is the highest in Europe, with the Matterhorn Glacier Paradise reaching 3,883 meters, offering unparalleled views and thrilling descents.

Zermatt is also famous for its excellent après-ski scene and mountain dining. Numerous on-piste restaurants, such as **Chez Vrony** and **Findlerhof**, offer delicious local cuisine and stunning views, making lunch breaks a memorable part of the day on the slopes.

The resort's state-of-the-art lift system ensures minimal wait times and efficient access to the diverse ski areas. The **Matterhorn Glacier Ride**, the world's highest 3S cable car, is a technological marvel that provides a swift and comfortable journey to the glacier ski area.

Overall, Zermatt's combination of extensive terrain, reliable snow, and top-notch amenities make it a top choice for skiing and snowboarding enthusiasts seeking a world-class alpine experience.

Hiking and Mountain Climbing

Zermatt is a hiker and mountaineer's paradise, offering a diverse range of trails and peaks that cater to all levels of ability and ambition. The region boasts over 400 kilometers of marked hiking trails, each providing stunning vistas of the Matterhorn and the surrounding Alpine landscape.

For casual hikers, the **Five Lakes Walk** is a must. This trail takes you past five picturesque mountain lakes, each reflecting the Matterhorn in its still waters. The route is well-marked and relatively easy, making it suitable for families and those looking for a leisurely hike. Another popular choice is the **Gornergrat Ridge Walk**, which offers panoramic views of the Gorner Glacier and a number of 4000-meter peaks.

Intermediate hikers will enjoy the challenge of the **Höhbalmen** trail, which rewards with spectacular views of the north face of the Matterhorn. This trail is more demanding, involving a significant elevation gain, but the breathtaking scenery and alpine flora along the way make it worthwhile.

For those seeking a more strenuous adventure, the **Europaweg** trail is a two-day trek that connects Zermatt with the nearby village of Grächen. This high-altitude route traverses dramatic landscapes, including the Charles Kuonen Suspension Bridge, the longest pedestrian suspension bridge in the world.

Mountain climbing in Zermatt is synonymous with the Matterhorn, one of the most iconic peaks in the Alps. Ascending the Matterhorn is a serious undertaking that requires technical skill and experience. Guided climbs are available for those looking to tackle this legendary mountain. Other notable climbs in the area include the Breithorn and the Weisshorn, both offering challenging routes and stunning summit views.

Zermatt's commitment to safety and sustainability is evident in the well-maintained trails, informative signposts, and the availability of mountain guides. Whether you're a casual hiker or an experienced climber, Zermatt provides a memorable alpine experience with its diverse trails and majestic peaks.

Exploring the Matterhorn and Other Natural Wonders

The Matterhorn, with its distinctive pyramid shape, is one of the most iconic mountains in the world and a symbol of the Swiss Alps. Exploring this natural wonder and the surrounding area offers an unforgettable experience for any visitor to Zermatt.

One of the best ways to get close to the Matterhorn is by taking the **Gornergrat Railway**. This historic cogwheel train journey offers panoramic views of the Matterhorn and the surrounding peaks as it ascends to the Gornergrat summit. At the top, visitors can enjoy breathtaking vistas, visit the observatory, and explore the marked trails that offer different perspectives of the Matterhorn.

For a more immersive experience, the **Matterhorn Glacier Paradise** is a must-visit. Accessible via the world's highest 3S cable car, this destination provides stunning views from 3,883 meters above sea level. The Glacier Palace, an ice grotto carved into the glacier, features ice sculptures and a tunnel network that allow visitors to walk beneath the glacier's surface.

Beyond the Matterhorn, Zermatt is surrounded by other natural wonders. The **Gorner Glacier**, the second-largest glacier in the Alps, can be explored from various viewpoints along the Gornergrat Ridge. The glacier's impressive ice formations and crevasses provide a dramatic landscape that is constantly changing.

The **Trift Gorge** is another remarkable natural attraction. A short hike from Zermatt leads to a suspension bridge spanning the gorge, offering thrilling views of the rushing waters below and the

rugged terrain. This area is particularly beautiful in
the spring and summer when the meltwater from
the glaciers is at its peak.

In the summer, the **Schwarzsee** area, located at
the base of the Matterhorn, offers tranquil alpine
meadows, clear lakes, and a network of hiking
trails. It's an ideal spot for picnicking and enjoying
the serene beauty of the Swiss Alps.

Exploring Zermatt's natural wonders, including the
Matterhorn, provides a profound appreciation of
the region's geological majesty and the dynamic
forces of nature that shape the landscape. Whether
through scenic train rides, high-altitude cable car
journeys, or immersive hikes, visitors are sure to be
captivated by the natural beauty and grandeur of
this alpine paradise.

Printed in Great Britain
by Amazon